Improve your GRAMMAR SKILLS

Susan Baing

OXFORD

253 Normanby Road, South Melbourne, Victoria 3205, Australia

Oxford University Press is a department of the University of Oxford. It furthers the University's objective of excellence in research, scholarship, and education by publishing worldwide in

Oxford New York

Auckland Cape Town Dar es Salaam Hong Kong Karachi Kuala Lumpur Madrid Melbourne Mexico City Nairobi New Delhi Shanghai Taipei Toronto

With offices in

Argentina Austria Brazil Chile Czech Republic France Greece Guatemala Hungary Italy Japan Poland Portugal Singapore South Korea Switzerland Thailand Turkey Ukraine Vietnam

OXFORD is a trademark of Oxford University Press in the UK and in certain other countries

First published 2002
Reprinted 2007
Reprinted 2009, 2010, 2014, 2015(D)

ISBN 978 0 19 551586 2.

Edited by Kate Deutrom and Paige Amor
Text and cover designed by Aileen Taylor
Illustrated by Melissa Webb
Typeset by Promptset Pty Ltd
Printed and bound in Australia by Ligare Book Printers, Pty Ltd

Contents

Overview—*Improve Your Grammar Skills*

Nouns and pronouns

Verbs

Adjectives and adverbs

Other useful words

Sentences

Please use your Oxford University Press Dictionary when required.
Answer all questions in your exercise book.

To the student

Grammar is the way in which words change themselves (for example, *walk* changes to *walked* in the past tense) and how they group together to make different kinds of sentences.

In the first part of this book you will learn about the parts of sentences. Sentences are made up of words that have different kinds of work to do. It is important to think about what work each word in a sentence does. This will help you understand sentences when you read them and when you write them yourself. Remember: sometimes a word that looks the same can do different kinds of work in a sentence. For example, *walk* can be a verb or a noun.

In the second part of this book you will learn about different kinds of sentences. You will see how all the words in sentences work together so that you can understand the sentence.

The answers to many of the exercises are at the back of the book. Always try to write your own sentences following the patterns in the exercises.

To the teacher

This book contains many rules for grammar, especially for the writing of correct sentences. It is important that your students write their own sentences to practice the constructions that are taught in the units.

Many of the rules are general and there are exceptions to them. However, it is best that your students understand the general rules first, and then when they are confident, they will find it easier to understand the exceptions to the rule.

Unit 1

Kinds of nouns

A noun is a name of a person, animal, place, thing, idea or feeling: *Tau* (person), *farmer* (person), *pig* (animal), *Daru* (place), *valley* (place), *canoe* (thing), *freedom* (idea), *joy* (feeling).

Activity A

Put a line under the nouns in these sentences. Each sentence has two nouns:

1 My <u>dog</u> likes to eat <u>kaukau</u>.
2 Gure goes to our school.
3 The teacher talked about Independence.
4 The river goes into the lake.
5 I used a hammer to build the box.
6 Lina saw the clouds.
7 Port Moresby is our capital.
8 The waves were big during the storm.
9 The highway has many trucks on it.
10 We start a new book on Monday.

Nouns can be divided into four groups: proper nouns, common nouns, abstract nouns and collective nouns.

Activity B

Proper nouns begin with a capital letter. They name people or places. Example: *I saw Sir Michael Somare in Wewak.*

1 Put a line under the proper nouns in this list:
Simbu, mountain, Monday, church, radio, Hani, Elizabeth, car, Toyota, banana, New Ireland, bus

2 Write six proper nouns to add to these lists:
Names you like: Sera, Lemba ...
Names for pets: Cedar, Blacky ...
Names of places you have visited: Tufi, Mendi ...
Days of the week: Monday ...

Activity C

Common nouns are the names of everyday things around us. Example: *The teacher told the student to leave his desk.* They do not begin with a capital letter unless they start a sentence.

1 Put a line under the common nouns on this list:
Madang, grass, cloud, forest, Dika, pencil, shark, boy, Tuesday, Coral Sea, paddle, cassowary, feather

2 Write six common nouns to add to each of these lists:
Food you like to eat: taro, ibika ...
Animals: shark, dog ...
Things you can see around you: desks, windows ...
Places you know about: river, beach ...
People: girl, headmaster ...

3 Common nouns name something you can see, hear, smell, taste and touch: *sea, wind, sand, kaukau.* Write some common nouns you have seen, to add to these lists:
Things I have seen today: road, plate, ...
Things I have heard today: radio, wind, ...
Things I have smelled today: frangipani, smoke, ...
Things I have touched today: hair, sandpaper, ...

Activity D

Abstract nouns name feelings or ideas. You can think of them, but you cannot see, hear, smell, taste or touch them. Example: *I listened with happiness and joy to the Bible story.*

1 Put a line under the abstract nouns on this list:
justice, Samuel, bicycle, fear, violence, road, attention, Port Moresby, freedom, crocodile, independence, love

2 Write an abstract noun from this list to complete the following sentences.
peace patience pain kindness excitement joy

a Lohia's broken finger gave him a lot of **p**_________.

b I could hear the **j**__________ in the congregation's voice as they sang the hymns.

c Nais enjoyed the **p**___________ and quiet of the village after the noise of Port Moresby.

d The Prime Minister's visit caused a lot of **e**______________.

e The nurse showed a lot of **k**_____________ to the sick child.

f We had to show a lot of **p**_____________ while we waited for the late plane.

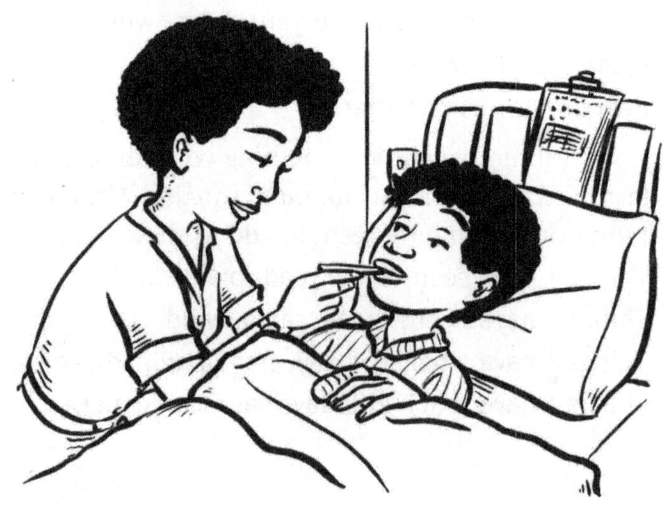

Activity E

Collective nouns name a group of people or things. Example: *The crowd cheered. Their team won.*

1 Put a line under the collective nouns on this list:
choir, singer, guitar, congregation, flock, committee, house, West New Britain, cat, queue, door

2 Write the collective nouns for these groups of things:
A ... of books.
A ... of flowers.
A ... of cattle.
A ... of soldiers.
A ... of dogs.

Activity F

Write your own lists of nouns that you have used in your writing, or seen in your reading. Sort them into the four groups: common, proper, abstract and collective nouns.

Unit 2

Singular and plural nouns

Singular nouns name one person, place or thing. Plural nouns name more than one person, place or thing.

Activity A

Most plural words are made by adding *s* to the singular word: *book–books, tree–trees.*

Make these singular nouns plural by adding *s*:

car, paddle, desk, book, bridge, teacher, cake, road, bat

Activity B

Nouns ending in *s, o, sh, ch, x* or *z*, add *es* to make the plural: *church–churches, box–boxes.*

Make these singular nouns plural by adding *es*:

match, brush, tax, fox, waltz, watch, church, potato, tomato, wish, pass, buzz, mix, gas, glass, class, hero, echo, volcano, mango, search

Activity C

Nouns that end in a consonant followed by *y* change the *y* to *i* and add *es*. Example: *baby–babies, fly–flies.*

Make these nouns plural by changing the *y* to *i* and adding *es*:

army, party, enemy, country, story, worry

Activity D

Nouns that end in a vowel (*a, e, i, o, u*) followed by *y* add *s* only: *monkey/monkeys*.

Make these nouns plural by adding *s*:

valley, key, bay, alley, chimney, boy, play, holiday, stingray, way, toy, tray

Activity E

Some nouns that end in *f* or *fe* change the *f* into *v* and add *es*: *knife/knives*.

Make these nouns plural by changing the *f* to *v* and adding *es*:

leaf, half, wharf, wolf, life, calf, thief, self, loaf, shelf

Activity F

Some words do not do any of these things: *child/children, sheep/sheep, scissors/scissors, man/men.*

Check your dictionary to find the plural of these nouns:

deer, foot, woman, tooth, mouse, louse, ox, aircraft

Activity G

Write the missing words:

1 One man, ten men	**7** One wolf, ten _______
2 One shell, ten _______	**8** One dwarf, ten _______
3 One house, ten _______	**9** One feather, ten _______
4 One child, ten _______	**10** One spoon, ten _______
5 One lolly, ten _______	**11** One glass, ten _______
6 One bus, ten _______	**12** One man, ten _______

Unit 3

Nouns you can count and nouns you can't count

Nouns you can count have a singular form and a plural form: *cat/cats, box/boxes.* Nouns you can't count do not have a plural form: *milk, tea.*

Activity A

Write some more nouns you can't count:

Food: rice ...	Raw materials: wood ...
Feelings: anger ...	Human qualities: strength ...
Things made up of small particles: milk ...	Many –ing forms: clothing ...

Activity B

When you write a sentence, *plural nouns* are followed by *plural verbs. Nouns you can't count* are followed by *singular verbs.* Write these sentences and put *is/are,* or *was/were* in the spaces.

Example: The coffee is sweet. (You can't count coffee.) The berries are ripe. (You can count berries.)

1 The tea ___________ hot.

2 The biscuits ___________ sweet.

3 The birds ___________ loud.

4 The cement ___________ set hard.

5 The team _________ winning.

6 The books ______________ hard to read.

7 Courage ________________ a good quality.

8 Letters ________________ fun to get.

9 Canoes ____________ used for fishing.

10 The sand ____________ smooth.

11 Steel ____________ very strong.

12 Smoking ____________ bad for you.

13 Running ____________ good exercise

14 The rice ____________ boiling.

15 The plates __________ clean.

Activity C

Many is used with nouns you can count. *Much* is used with nouns you can't count. Write *many* or *much* in the spaces.

Example: Many leaves, much rain.

1_____ happiness	9_____ sisters
2_____ facts	10_____ women
3_____ coffee	11_____ children
4_____ patience	12_____ chocolates
5_____ museums	13_____ sugar
6_____ trust	14_____ ice cream
7_____ wood	15_____ furniture
8_____ novels	

Unit 4

Pronouns

Pronouns take the place of nouns. They are used instead of repeating the names of people, places or things.

Example: *The man saw the dog. The man gave the dog some food.* We write this instead: *The man saw the dog. He gave it some food.*

Activity A

Underline the pronouns in these sentences:

1 As Gia got off the bus, she heard the school bell ring.

2 The bell sounded like it was angry.

3 She ran towards the classroom door.

4 It was closed.

5 The teacher was already there. She frowned at Gia.

Activity B

Pronouns are used when we are the person speaking: *I*/we or *me*/*us.*

Example: I went to school early.

Sangi came with me.

We got there on time.

Segi saw us.

Look at each of the following sentences. Write your own sentence to follow the pattern:

1 I opened my book.

2 The teacher asked me to read.

3 We all listened to the story.

4 The teacher told us to write our own stories.

Activity C

Pronouns are used when we are speaking to others: *you* (singular), *you* (plural).

Example: You should clean the blackboard, John.

"Listen, class, I am talking to you."

Write the pronoun *you* in the space:

1 "Will _____ clean the blackboard, please, Anna," asked the teacher.

2 I will send _____ a letter soon.

3 Do _________all like writing stories?

4 All of _______ can write a story for me.

5 I want _______ to get some firewood, please, Kevana.

6 "Listen, class," said the teacher, "_____ are going to go outside and wait for me there."

Activity D

Pronouns are used when we are speaking about someone: *he, him, she, her, they, them*

Example: He arrived early.

Gia looked at him.

She was very late.

The teacher gave the book to her.

They arrived a bit later.

The teacher was angry with them.

Look at each sentence. Write a sentence to follow the pattern.

1 She wore a skirt to school.

2 He helped his mother.

3 His father gave him a new shirt.

4 She helped her cousin do the homework.

5 The students ran because they were late.

6 The headmaster punished them.

Pronouns are used to show who owns something:

This book is *mine*. (*mine* stands for *my book*)
That house is *ours*. (*ours* stands for *our house*)
That book is *yours*. (*yours* stands for *your book*)
The cat is *his*. (*his* stands for *his cat*)
The dog is *hers*.(*hers* stands for *her dog*)
The truck is *theirs*. (*theirs* stands for *their truck*)

Activity E

Underline the pronouns that show who owns the nouns in the sentences:

Example: "Is this book yours?" the teacher asked.

1 "No," I replied. "Mine is in the desk."
2 He then asked the other students if the book was theirs.
3 "No," they said, "ours are on the shelf."
4 Nobody knew who the book belonged to. Gia came late. When she saw the book, she said it might be hers.
5 Then, a boy said it was his.
6 "Oh," said the teacher, "so it is yours."

Activity F

Write what the pronoun stands for in each of these sentences:

1 Is this shoe hers? (*her shoe*)
2 Is the pen yours? (your ...)
3 That classroom is newer then ours. (our ...)
4 That library book is his. (his ...)
5 We said the rubbish was ours. (our ...)
6 They said the truck was theirs (their ...)
7 Is this desk hers? (her ...)
8 I said that the torn shirt was mine. (my ...)

9 Is that pen <u>his</u>? (his ...)
10 That rice is <u>mine</u>. (my ...)
11 That plate is <u>yours</u>. (your ...)
12 The coffee plantation is <u>theirs</u>. (their ...)

Activity G

Write a paragraph about your class. Use as many pronouns as you can. Check to make sure the reader can tell which noun your pronouns stand for. Here is the first sentence of the paragraph:

A strange thing happened in our class today ...

Unit 5

Using *I* and *me* correctly

When to use *I* in a sentence:

Look at the two sentences. Which is right?
Mitieli and I went to the river. Mitieli and me went to the river.

To find out, make the sentence into two sentences:
Mitieli went to the river. I went to the river.
Mitieli went to the river. Me went to the river.

Now you can see which sentence is correct.
The correct sentence is: *Mitieli and I went to the river.*

Activity A

Write *I* or *me* to complete the sentence. Check your answer by looking at the two sentences.

1 Gadoeno and ______ raced to the fence.
Gadoeno raced to the fence. I raced to the fence.
Gadoeno raced to the fence. Me raced to the fence.

2 Samson and ______ played football.
Samson and played football. I played football.
Samson played football. Me played football.

3 Laros and ______ went to the garden.
Laros went to the garden. I went to the garden.
Laros went to the garden. Me went to the garden.

4 Eli and ______ helped the teacher.
Eli helped the teacher. I helped the teacher.
Eli helped the teacher. Me helped the teacher.

When to use *me* in a sentence:

Look at the two sentences. Which is right?

Amatu gave the mango to Pato and me. Amatu gave the mango to Pato and I. To find out, make the sentence into two sentences:
Amatu gave the mango to Pato. Amatu gave the mango to me.
Amatu gave the mango to Pato. Amatu gave the mango to I.

Now you can see which sentence is correct.
The correct sentence is: *Amatu gave the mango to Pato and me.*

Activity B

Write *I* or *me* in the space. Check your answer by looking at the two sentences.

1 The dog sat next to Leilani and _____.

The dog sat next to Leilani. The dog sat next to me.

The dog sat next to Leilani. The dog sat next to I.

2 The man got angry with Bau and ______.

The man got angry with Bau. The man got angry with me.

The man got angry with Bau. The man got angry with I.

3 Seri gave a pawpaw to Kias and _______.

Seri gave a pawpaw to Kias. Seri gave a pawpaw to me.

Seri gave a pawpaw to Kias. Seri gave a pawpaw to I.

4 The pig ran towards Jeffrey and _____.

The pig ran towards Jeffrey. The pig ran towards me.

The pig ran towards Jeffrey. The pig ran towards I.

Unit 6

Kinds of verbs

Verbs tell you what is happening in sentences.

Most verbs are action verbs	She ran down the road.
Some verbs are saying verbs	She spoke to me.
Some verbs are thinking verbs	I know the way to school.
Some verbs are being verbs	She is clever.
Some verbs are having verbs	She has the answer.

Activity A

Write an *action verb* to finish the sentences. Choose from these verbs: cleaned, peeled, won, played, paddled, jumped.

1 Sera _____ the race.	4 Mother ____ the taro.
2 Sigin ____ the guitar.	5 Mare ____ over the gate.
3 Kapi ____ the canoe.	6 The girls ___ the yard.

Now write your own sentences with action verbs.

Activity B

Write a *saying verb* to finish the sentences. Choose from these verbs: hissed, yelled, asked, laughed, spoke, warned.

1 The teacher __________ loudly.

2 The snake __________ at me.

3 Father __________ us not to go near the flooded river.

4 The children __________ loudly for their team.

5 We _____________ what the price of the bread was.

Now write your own sentences with saying verbs.

Activity C

Write a thinking verb to finish the sentences. Choose from these verbs: knew, worried, enjoyed, understood, believed.

1 The boy ______ about his sick mother.

2 The teacher ______ the student's lies.

3 We all _______ the new books.

4 The girl ______ how to make a bilum.

5 The class _____ the lesson.

Now write your own sentences with thinking verbs.

Activity D

Write a *being verb* to finish these sentences. Choose from these parts of the being verb: *am, is, are.*

1 I _______________ happy today.

2 This ibika _______________ delicious.

3 My favourite teacher _______________ Mr Tapura.

4 The kaukau ________ cooked.

5 We ___________ ready to do our writing.

Write a *having verb* to finish these sentences. Choose from these parts of the having verb: *has, have.*

1 We ___________ old books.

2 Our uniforms ___________ buttons.

3 My cap ___________ a picture on it.

4 Our truck ____________ a flat tyre.

5 Jimmy _________ a new dog.

Unit 7

Helping verbs

Some verbs work together in a sentence. When a verb works with another verb it is called a *helping verb*. Here are some helping verbs:
do, does, did
can, could
will, would
shall, should
am, are, is, was, were
have, has, had.

Helping verbs are useful for making questions. The helping verb is separated from the main verb:
<u>Can</u> (helping verb) *you <u>swim</u>* (main verb)*?*
<u>Do</u> (helping verb) *you <u>like</u>* (main verb) *mangoes?*

Activity A

Put a line under the *helping verb* in each sentence. Then write a sentence that follows the pattern.

Examples: Nenci <u>can</u> run fast.

Segi can talk loudly.

1 When do you start your new job?

2 Does Heni like going to school?

3 Did they leave early?

4 I can run fast.

5 Can we eat the mangoes?

6 The tyre could burst.

7 Shall we eat now?

8 Should we shut the window?

9 Students should wear uniforms.
10 We will read that book.
11 He would read everyday.
12 Would you like an orange to eat?
13 I am doing my homework.
14 Are you washing the windows?
15 Is Sangi chopping the wood?

16 It was getting late.
17 The dogs were running down the road.
18 Have you forgotten your book?
19 Serah has finished her food.
20 My mother had prepared rice.
21 I am weeding the garden
22 Can you go to the store?
23 He was going to Goroka.
24 Are you singing in the band?
25 The rascal could go to jail.
26 The girls were going to church.
27 I shall help the old women.
28 Did you kill the pig?
29 She has gone to the library.
30 The doctor is working at the hospital.

Unit 8

Verb tenses

You use verbs to write about something that is happening now, or in the past, or in the future. This is called the tense of a verb. *I kick the ball.* (present tense) *I kicked the ball.* (past tense) *I will kick the ball tomorrow.* (future tense)

Activity A

Look at the verb in the brackets and write it in the sentence.

Example: He __________ his lunch to school. (bring) He brings his lunch to school.

1 I __________ in the evening. (read)
2 Who __________ homework? (like)
3 We __________ fish. (eat)
4 Sumpu __________ football well. (play)
5 Reggie __________ an eagle. (see)
6 The boy __________ his mother. (thank)
7 The dog __________ at strangers. (bark)
8 The bus __________ to Lae each day. (travel)
9 I __________ to school. (walk)
10 The bus __________ outside the school. (stop)

Activity B

Some verbs add *-ed*, to show the verb is in the past tense. Look at the verb in the brackets and write it in the sentence.

Example: Gabi __________very well yesterday. (play) Gabi played very well yesterday.

1 Bangu __________ the most goals. (kick)

2 Ranua __________ two goals. (stop)

3 Hapu __________ on the mud. (slip)

4 The referee __________ the end of the match. (call)

5 The boys __________ for us. (cheer)

6 The dog __________ at the ball. (bark)

7 Mother __________ the soup. (stir)

8 I __________ the envelope. (address)

9 We __________ the bus driver. (thank)

10 Last night we __________ a video. (watch)

Activity C

Look at the verb in the brackets and write the verb in the sentence. Put *will* in front of the verb.

Example: I __________for Lae in the morning. (leave)
I will leave for Lae in the morning.

1 The students __________ tea at lunchtime. (drink)

2 I __________ the drawing. (copy)

3 My friend __________ to my letter soon. (reply)

4 We __________ up early tomorrow. (wake)

5 The teacher __________ us a story soon. (tell)

6 The ripe mangoes __________ from the tree. (drop)

7 The bell __________ at 7:30. (ring)

8 I __________ to my grandfather. (speak)

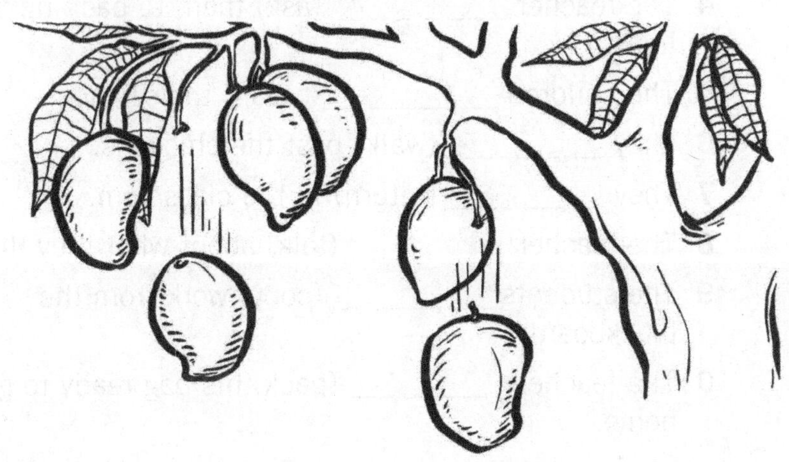

Unit 9

Using *has*, *have* and *had* with verbs

Using has and have with verbs.

You add *have* or *has* to the past tense verb to show that the action of the verb has finished.

Example: *She has started the weeding.* (*has* + *started*) Has is used with single nouns or pronouns.
We have started the weeding. (*have* + *started*) Have is used with plural nouns and pronouns.

Activity A

Put *has* or *have* and the past tense verb in these sentences:

Example: Kila __________ (finish) his homework. Kila has finished his homework.

1 The students __________ (finish) planting the peanuts.

2 They __________ (cover) each seed with soil.

3 They __________ (plant) peanuts here since the school opened.

4 The teacher __________ (ask) them to pack up the tools.

5 The children __________ (wash) their hands.

6 They __________ (walk) past the chickens.

7 They __________ (return) to the classroom.

8 The teacher __________ (talk) about what they did.

9 The students __________ (copy) work from the blackboard.

10 The teacher __________ (pack) his bag ready to go home.

Using had with verbs.

You add *had* to the past tense verb to show that one action was finished before the other.

Example: *We had finished the weeding before the bell rang.* (We finished weeding first, then the bell rang later.)

Activity B

Put *had* and the past tense verb in these sentences:

Example: I __________ (wash) the clothes before it rained. I had washed the clothes before it rained.

1 The students __________ (harvest) the peanuts before the rain fell.

2 They __________ (pick) the nuts off the plants by the time it started to rain.

3 After we __________ (wash) the peanuts, we put them in a bag.

4 We __________ (finish) our work early, so we left.

5 After the rain __________ (start) we ran into the classroom.

6 He __________ (plant) a new garden before the wet season began.

7 We __________ (walk) to the shop before it got dark.

8 They __________ (play) their match before lunch.

9 Before I saw my marks, I __________ (worry) about the test.

10 After it __________ (rain), the sky cleared.

Unit 10

Using *-ing* verbs

Look at these sentences: *The Grade 7s are weeding the garden. The Grade 8s are cutting the grass. Are you working on the exercises? I'm not helping you.* You use *-ing* verbs when you write about something that is happening *at the very moment*. The form of this verb is: *am/is/are + -ing verb.*
I am writing./I'm writing.
She is writing./She's writing.
They/We/You are writing. They're/We're/You're writing.

Activity A

Write *is/are + -ing* verbs in these sentences.

Example: We ______ ________ (sit) at our desks.
We are sitting at our desks.

1 Gabi ____ ________ (draw) a picture.
2 I ____ ________ (watch) him.
3 Laka _____ ________ (fold) some paper.
4 Dawe and Matti _____ ________ (scrape) a coconut.
5 The cockatoo ____ ________ (sit) on the branch.

Now write some sentences of your own.

Activity B

Write *am/is/are +ing* verbs in these sentences.

1 The family ____ ________ (sit) on the veranda of their house. Tau is downstairs.
2 "What ____ you ______ (do) downstairs, Tau?" asked Father.

3 "I'____ ________ (wash) the dog, Dad."

4 "____ your sister ________ (help) you?"

5 "No, Dad, she'__ ____ (sit) on the steps with Laka, as usual."

Look at these sentences: *The Grade 7s were weeding the garden. The Grade 8s were cutting the grass. Were you working on the exercises? I wasn't helping you.* You use *-ing* verbs when you write about something that was going on in the past. The form of this verb is *was/were + -ing verb.*
I was writing. They were writing.

Activity C

Write the *was/were + -ing* verbs in this passage:

Yesterday evening I [1]____ ________ (sit) on my veranda. I [2]____ ________ (watch) the family next door.

The father [3]____ ________ (rest) upstairs, while his son Tau [4]____ ________ (wash) the dog downstairs. The father [5]____ ________ (ask) his son what he [6]____ ________ (do). The daughter and her friend Laka[7] ____ ___ (sit) on the steps.

Soon I saw that my neighbour [8]_____ _____ (come) downstairs, so I went over to join him.

Activity D

Write some sentences of your own like the sentences in Activity C.

Unit 11

Making the nouns and verbs agree

Nouns and verbs in sentences must agree (match). If the noun or pronoun is singular, then the verb is singular. If the noun or pronoun is plural, then the verb is plural.

Example: *The boy likes science.* (singular noun [boy] and singular verb [likes]) *The boys like science.* (plural noun [boys] and plural verb [like]) *She likes science.* (singular pronoun [she] and singular verb[likes]) *They like science.* (plural pronoun [they] and plural verb [like])

Activity A

Write the singular verb for a singular noun and the plural verb for a plural noun:

Example: The dogs ________ (bites/bite) the bones. The dogs bite the bones.

1 The children __________ (go/goes) fishing often.
2 One girl __________ (feel/feels) very lucky.
3 Temu __________ (catch/catches) the most fish.
4 The other boys and girls don't ______ (think/thinks) this is fair.
5 The canoe ______ (speed/speeds) through the water.
6 The waves ___________ (look/looks) small.
7 The sun ___________ (shine/shines) from a clear sky.
8 No clouds __________ (stop/stops) the sun's rays.
9 The paddles __________ (make/makes) little splashes.
10 The children ____ (throw/throws) the net near the reef.
11 The boys ________ (pull/pulls) the net in.
12 The net _________ (feel/feels) heavy.

Activity B

Write the singular verb for a singular pronoun and the plural verb for the plural pronoun. Look at this table carefully before you start. All the verbs are in the present tense:

Pronoun	**she he it**	**I**	**you they we**
Verb	is	am	are
Verb	does has	do have	do have

1 They __________ (am/are) getting ready to go fishing.
2 I __________ (am/are) ready.
3 Do you think she ________ (has/have) a knife?
4 __________ (Do/Does) it look like rain?
5 __________ (Are/ Is) the waves rough?
6 They __________ (hasn't/haven't) caught any fish.
7 We __________ (have/has) a full net.
8 I __________ (is/am) ready to go home.
9 You __________ (are/am) a good fisherman.
10 You all __________ (have/has) a share of the catch.
11 It __________ (is/are) time to clean the fish.
12 They __________ (is/are) tired.

Unit 12

Irregular verbs

Some verbs do not follow a regular pattern. Example:
I swim everyday. (present tense)
She swims everyday. (present tense)
I swam everyday. (past tense)
I will swim everyday. (future tense)
I have swum everyday. (helping verb *have*)
I had swum everyday. (helping verb *had*)
I am swimming everyday. (helping verb *be*)
I was swimming everyday. (helping verb *was*)

Activity A

Write in the correct verb forms. Use your dictionary to check you have the correct forms.

1 speak

I __________ to her everyday. (present tense)

She __________ to her everyday. (present tense)

I __________ to her everyday. (past tense)

I will __________ to her everyday. (future tense)

I have __________ to her everyday. (helping verb have)

2 catch

I __________ fish everyday. (present tense)

She __________ fish everyday. (present tense)

I __________ fish everyday. (past tense)

I will __________ fish everyday. (future tense)

I have __________ fish everyday. (helping verb have)

3 cut

I __________ grass everyday. (present tense)

She __________ grass everyday. (present tense)

I __________ grass everyday. (past tense)

I will __________ grass everyday. (future tense)

I have __________ grass everyday. (helping verb have)

4 write

I __________ letters everyday. (present tense)

She __________ letters everyday. (present tense)

I __________ letters everyday. (past tense)

I will __________ letters everyday. (future tense)

I have __________ letters everyday. (helping verb have)

Activity B

Write the verbs on this table. Use your dictionary to check you have the correct forms.

present	past	have + past
find	found	have found
choose	chose	have chosen
hit	hit	have hit
come		
see		
bend		
feel		
kneel		
leave		
sleep		
shut		

show		
buy		
bring		
freeze		
forget		

Activity C

Underline the verbs in these sentences and then write your own sentence to follow the pattern.

1 Last week I found a special kind of frog.

2 I had forgotten to tell my mother about the frog.

3 My mother came home.

4 She saw the frog on the table.

5 She shut the frog up in a box.

6 I thought the cat had eaten the frog.

Activity D

The verb *to be* has many different forms:

I am, you are, she is, it is, they are, we are (present tense)

I was, you were, she was, it was, they were (past tense)

I will be, you will be, she will be, it will be, they will be (future tense).

Follow the instruction about tense, and write the sentences using a form of the verb *to be*:

1 They will be running in the race. (future)

2 It __________ rainy last week. (past)

3 I __________ the winner last year. (past)

4 You __________ happy when you win. (future)

5 I __________ a fast runner. (present)

6 Jonas __________ the team captain. (present)

7 They __________ cheering us. (past)

8 The teachers __________ sitting in the shade. (past)

9 They ___________ happy with the result. (present)

10 I ____________ leaving tomorrow.(future)

11 Lena ______________ sorry. (past)

12 She ______________ there soon. (future)

13 It ______________ hot yesterday. (past)

14 It ______________ hot again today. (future)

15 You ____________ sorry. (past)

Activity E

Write a story about your school with different forms of the verb to be. Example: *Last year I was at the school near the river, but this year I am at the new school on the hill.*

Unit 13

Adjectives

Adjectives are describing words that tell more about nouns or pronouns. You can describe nouns and pronouns by telling about their …

colour: red, black, yellow
size: small, large
number or amount: fifteen, many
age: old, youthful
taste: spicy, hot
weight: heavy, light,
direction: north
quality: beautiful, careless, happy

Activity A

Write a list of nouns and the adjectives that describe them:

Example: *black* dog, *pretty* girl, *endless* story

Adjectives	Nouns
black, pretty, wide, tall, faithful, wobbly, endless, dangerous, two, tragic, faded, bored, wonderful, golden, wooden, smoky, friendly, lonely, blunt, ten, several, fierce, clean, terrible, careless, dark, safe, strange	building, team, night, fight, dog, weather, bridge, mother, match, decoration, driver, story, knife, truck, valley, river, teacher, classroom, girl, library, dormitory, medal, sky, tree, flavour, mixture, fire, cat, climate, volcano, book, canoe

Activity B

Find the adjectives in these sentences and put a line under them. Put a circle around the nouns that the adjectives describe.

1 The tiny frog was hiding in the dry leaves.
2 We ran towards the sandy path.
3 My mother cooked some delicious scones.
4 We learnt about our traditional trade.
5 The old man came to tell us about making stone axes.
6 The ripe mango fell to the hard ground.
7 The heavy bilum was full of cut firewood.
8 The students were digging the large gardens.
9 The salty soup was thrown away.
10 The north wind brought heavy rain.

Activity C

Put an adjective in each column to describe the noun:

Number	Size	Shape	Colour	Noun
three	huge	long	grey	pigs
				books
				trees
				taro
				crabs
				crocodiles
				shirts
				pencils
				bananas
				arrows

Unit 14

Comparing using adjectives

Adjectives change when you use them to compare nouns and pronouns. *-er* or *more* is used when two things are compared. *-est* or *most* is used when more than two things are being compared. Example: *I am taller than my sister. I am more beautiful than my sister. My brother is the tallest in our family. He is the most careful.*

Activity A

Most short adjectives add *-er* when two things are compared. Write these sentences using the correct form of the adjective:

1 The game was _________ today than last week. (long)
2 Gabi ran __________ than Sepou. (fast)
3 The other team was ___________ than us. (slow)
4 The oval was __________ than last year. (smooth)
5 The noise became __________ . (loud)

Activity B

Most long adjectives add *more* to the adjective when two things are being compared. Write these sentences using the correct form of the adjective:

1 Running is ___________ than walking. (tiring)
2 The path was __________ after the rain (slippery)
3 His job is __________ than mine. (dangerous)
4 That tree is __________ than the one we saw yesterday. (enormous)
5 The boy looked __________ than his friend. (puzzled)

Activity C

When more than two things are being compared, short adjectives usually add *the* + *-est* to the adjective. Write these sentences using the correct form of the adjective:

1 My father is __________ in our family. (thin)

2 My grandfather is __________ . (wise)

3 My sister is __________ . (pretty)

4 My brother is __________ . (strong)

5 My mother is __________ . (clever)

6 As for me, I am just __________ . (noisy)

Activity D

When more than two things are being compared, long adjectives usually put *the* + *most* in front of the adjective. Write these sentences using the correct form of the adjective:

1 My cousin is __________ girl in the class. (intelligent)

2 My aunty is ________ woman in the village. (beautiful)

3 My grandfather is ________ man in the clan. (powerful)

4 My grandmother cooks _______ food. (wonderful)

5 My uncle is _______ man in the show. (handsome)

6 My father is __________. (honest)

Activity E

Write a story about your family. Use adjectives, which compare two things, and adjectives, which compare more than two things.

Unit 15

Adverbs

Adverbs tell something about verbs. They tell *how*: badly, softly, beautifully, gently, easily, quickly. *She swam quickly.* (how: *quickly*) They tell *how often*: always, often, never, sometimes. *She always swims.* (how often: *always*) They tell *when*: during, yesterday, last night, at night, today. *She will swim today.* (when: *today*) They tell *where*: there, everywhere, here, next to, near to. *She will swim there.* (where: *there*)

Activity A

Write any adverbs that are in each sentence:

1 My friend and I walked slowly to the beach. slowly

2 We always go to the beach on Saturday. ________

3 It was cold, so we ran quickly into the water. ________

4 My friend cut his foot badly on a sharp shell. ________

5 We had to leave early. ________

6 I called softly to my friend. ________

7 The books were put down everywhere. ________

8 We sometimes swim when it is cold. ________

Activity B

Write adverbs in these sentences. Follow the instructions in the brackets:

1 We went to the library. (when did we go?) We went to the library yesterday.

2 We borrow books. (how often do we borrow?)

3 The teacher spoke to us. (how did she speak?)

4 We should sit down. (where should we sit down?)

5 The bananas grew. (how did they grow?)

6 We visited my grandmother. (when did you visit?)

7 We go to visit her. (how often do you go?)

8 Grandmother was sitting. (where was she sitting?)

Activity C

Adverbs can be used for comparing. *He sang loudly. I sang more loudly. Davai sang the most loudly of all. Sigi ran quickly. Gabi ran less quickly. Sabine ran the least quickly.*

Write sentences to finish these comparisons:

1 Sigiri wrote badly.

2 Albert spoke softly.

3 Kia swam slowly.

4 Tano played roughly.

5 Hari laughed excitedly.

Activity D

Find six adverbs in the square. Each adverb should end in the **ly** shown in the centre of the square.

s	l	o	a	d
r	q	f	o	u
b	o	ly	u	t
s	o	g	i	c
w	u	h	d	k

Unit 16

Prepositions

Many prepositions tell about time or place. Some prepositions that tell about place are: *in, on, under, over, across, behind, past, down, near, into, at, on top, next to, in between, opposite, among, through, outside.* Some prepositions that tell about time are: *during, before, after, until, since, at midday, at night, then, for (an hour), on (Thursday).* Prepositions are always followed by nouns or pronouns: *on the shelf, beneath my clothes.*

Activity A

Look at the example of the cats and the tree. Draw a desk, a truck and a canoe in your book. Draw some cats near them and write prepositions to show where they are.

Activity B

Write the prepositions in this paragraph that show *place.* The first one has been underlined for you.

An old woman lived <u>in</u> a bush hut in the forest. The hut was beside a river, between two hills. All the children were too frightened to go near the hut. They thought they could see the old woman watching them through the door, when they went fishing among the rocks. They used to hide behind the bushes. They thought she never came outside her house.

Activity C

Write the prepositions in this paragraph that show *time.* The first one has been underlined for you.

One day, <u>before</u> the sun was up, two girls left their house to go fishing. During the day, they took no notice of the old woman watching them. They fished for the whole day, until late afternoon. Then, they noticed the old woman had crept near them. They left the fish and ran for home before dark. They didn't go back for a week.

Activity D

Finish each sentence by choosing the missing preposition from the list:

1 Taku likes to swim _______ the river.	beneath
2 We drank the water _______ the day.	before
3 Bats fly _________.	in
4 We ate, _______ went to bed.	since
5 Sigin travels _______ canoe each day.	by
6 I have lived in Madang ________ 1998.	then
7 Patapu finds fish ________ the rocks.	during
8 We are not allowed ________ the road.	from
9 The river flows ________ the mountain.	across
10 The children ate _________ they slept.	at night

Unit 17

Connecting words

Connecting words join words and groups of words.

Activity A

Connecting words like *and*, *so*, *or* and *but* join the same kind of words or groups of words. Example: *We caught fish and crabs.* Put a line under the connecting words in these sentences:

> Our favourite food is kaukau and wing-bean. Our mother knows this, so she cooks them often. We also like fresh fish, but we know fish is hard to get here. We like to take pineapple slices or mangoes to school for lunch.

Activity B

Write these sentences with the connecting words shown:

1 The day was damp ________ cloudy. (and)

2 We had the choice of going to the beach ________ staying at home. (or)

3 We love the beach _____ we decided to go there. (so)

4 We played in the water _______ sand. (and)

5 We went home tired ______ happy. (but)

Activity C

Write these sentences with a connecting word. Choose from *and*, *so*, *but*, *or*

1 Would you like to swim ________ sit on the sand?

2 After the race, we were exhausted _____ satisfied.

3 The day was cloudy ________ hot.

4 The water was warm ________ calm.

5 We were tired _______ hungry.

Activity D

Some connecting words are used to join parts of sentences: *because, unless, before, whenever, since, although, if, until, so that.* Example: *It rains <u>whenever</u> we plan a picnic.* Find the connecting words in the following sentences:

1 We ran because we wanted to spend as much time as possible at the beach.

2 It rained before we got to the beach.

3 Since we wanted to swim, we didn't take any notice.

4 We left our towels and food under a canoe so that they would keep dry.

5 Unless it rained heavily, we would stay at the beach.

Activity E

Join the two parts of the sentence with the connecting words shown in brackets.

1 We go to the beach everyday. It rains. (unless)

2 We are happy. The weather is fine. (if)

3 We walk to the beach. We have breakfast. (after)

4 We hurry. We'll have more time at the beach. (so that)

5 My oldest sister comes too. She needs to look after us. (because)

6 We stay at the beach. It gets dark. (until)

> Connecting words join short sentences and make writing more interesting. You can also start a sentence with a connecting word. Connecting words tell you the reason, place or time.

Activity F

Some connecting words show the reason why something happened. Example: *We were late to school because the buses were not running.* OR *Because the buses were not running, we were late for school.* Join these sentences using *because*:

1 The headmaster was angry. We were late.

2 We missed the first half of the test. The students had already started it.

3 We could not finish. We didn't have enough time.

4 I felt upset. I thought I would fail the test.

5 The teacher said we could sit the test again. Many students had been late.

6 I passed the test. I had studied very hard.

7 My parents were pleased. My marks were good.

8 I was allowed to go to Daru. I had worked hard.

Activity G

Connecting words such as *wherever* or *where* are used to show the place. Example: *We put the newspaper where he could see it. Bats gather wherever they can find fruit to eat.* Write these sentences using the connecting word shown in brackets.

1 I stood there. I could see the ocean. (where)

2 Birds feed on seed. They can find it. (wherever)

3 This is the place. I saw a crocodile. (where)

4 Weeds will grow. There is an open space. (wherever)

5 I hung up the wet clothes. They could get dry. (where)

6 That is the place. We got off the bus. (where)

7 I planted flowers. There was space in my garden. (wherever)

8 The PMV picks up people. The people wait. (wherever)

Activity H

Connecting words such as *after, before, when, whenever* and *while* show time. Example: *I cleaned the house* while *my sister went shopping.* Write these sentences using the connecting word shown in brackets.

1 My sister came home. She finished the shopping. (after)
2 She saw Henoa. She was on the bus. (when)
3 She asked Henoa to come and visit. Henoa was in the neighbourhood. (whenever)
4 She put away the food. She made the tea. (before)
5 We drank the cup of tea. We put the food in the cupboard. (after)
6 I peeled kaukau. My sister scraped the coconut. (while)
7 I eat a lot of bananas. They have been cooked in coconut milk. (whenever)
8 We washed the plates. We went to the garden. (before)

Unit 18

What is a sentence?

A sentence is a group of words that makes sense on its own. Look at these examples: *I see a truck. The truck belongs to the school. Who is driving the truck? Stop the truck!*

Some groups of words are not sentences. Look at these examples. *Waiting for the school truck.* (Who is waiting?) *Late as always.* (Who or what is late?) *When the truck is late.* (What happens when the truck is late?) These groups of words are not sentences. Something important has been left out.

Activity A

Write *yes* if you think the group of words is a sentence and *no,* if you think it is not a sentence.

1 The prefect is angry.
2 When you are angry.
3 My dog is getting old.
4 Most weekends we play sport.
5 Running out of petrol.
6 The truck broke down.
7 Going on the bus.
8 When you reach the road.
9 After that, you walk along the path.
10 We often go on the bus.
11 All of us.
12 Many friends.

13 Please help your sister with the cooking.
14 By the river.
15 Have you seen Tau?

Activity B

Join these groups of words to write sentences. Example: *Interesting book* is <u>not</u> a sentence. We join it to *This is an* to make a sentence: *This is an interesting book.*

1 When you are angry. (I don't like it)
2 At the gate. (she waited)
3 The crocodile! (look out for)
4 Going on the bus. (we like)
5 Delicious food. (my mother cooks)
6 My dog. (I like to play with)
7 Where the road ends. (get off the bus)
8 Going home. (he is)
9 A new pen friend. (I have)
10 Under the mango tree. (I sat)

Activity C

Write proper sentences of your own, using these groups of words. You can make them into a little story:

at the gate	for the last time
waving sadly	going home
onto the bus	made of sago leaves
on a seat	food for the journey

Unit 19

Kinds of sentences

The kinds of sentences are as follows:
Statement: *The student is clever.* Question: *Why is Tau late?* Order or request: *Leave the book closed.* Exclamation: *You're late!*

Activity A

The statement sentence begins with a capital letter and ends with a full stop. Write two more sentences like these sentences:

1 The store is closed.

2 I believe in studying hard.

3 Mangoes are my favourite fruit.

Activity B

Questions ask something. They begin with a capital letter and end with a question mark. Write each statement sentence as a question. Example: *Sepou feels sick. Does Sepou feel sick? The store is closed. Is the store closed?*

1 Tau's dog is old.	**5** The food is ready.
2 Gia lives there.	**6** You are frightened.
3 Lohia reads a lot.	**7** You eat tin fish.
4 The bus is late.	**8** You like mangoes.

Activity C

Orders or requests start with a capital letter and usually end in a full stop. Look at each sentence and write some similar sentences of your own.

1 Kila, drop the ball.
2 Turn right at the trade store.
3 Look out for that snake.
4 You need to run towards the goal.
5 Pass me that bilum, please.

Activity D

An exclamation expresses feeling. It ends with an exclamation mark. Example: *Don't you dare talk to Tau like that! What a hot day! That hurt me!* Write five more exclamation sentences.

Activity E

Look at each sentence and write if it is a statement, question, order or exclamation.

1 Are you going on the school trip?
2 The trip will visit the chicken farm.
3 Chicken farming is hard work.
4 Shut the door.
5 The chickens have escaped!
6 Please catch the chickens.
7 Would you like to take this one home?
8 There's a chicken on the bus!
9 Get that chicken off the bus.
10 Will I cook the chicken now?

Unit 20

The two parts of sentences

Birds fly. This is a sentence. The sentence has two parts. *Birds* is *the subject*. The subject tells you who or what is doing something. It is a noun or pronoun. It is the naming part of the sentence. *Fly* is *the predicate*. The predicate tells you what is happening. It is the telling part of the sentence.

Follow these steps to find the subject and the predicate:
Read the sentence: *Young dogs play all day.*
Find the verb: play
Ask the question <u>who</u> or <u>what</u> to find the verb.
The answer is the subject: *young dogs.*
The rest of the sentence is the predicate: *play all day.*

Activity A

A sentence must have a verb. To find the verb, try seeing if it makes sense after *he* or *she*. Example: *He slept.* (verb) *She laughed.* (verb) *It hot.* (not a verb) *He funny.* (not a verb) The words *hot* and *funny* do not make sense after he or she, so they are not verbs. Write if each word following *he* or *she* is a verb:

1 She is over there.

2 He over.

3 She warmly.

4 She plays the piano.

5 He right.

6 He fell.

7 She likes gospel music.

8 He guitar player.

Activity B

Put a line under the subject in each sentence. Put a circle around the verb. Follow the steps in the box on the previous page. The first one has been done for you.

1 My grandfather (took) us for a walk in the bush.

2 Birds were calling.

3 Butterflies flew in the branches of the trees.

4 A bird of paradise was singing.

5 Rain suddenly started to fall.

6 We ran for shelter under a ficus tree.

7 The stream was flooded very quickly.

8 The path was very muddy on the way home.

Activity C

Match each subject with a predicate and write the sentence.

Subject	Predicate
1 The rain	is ready.
2 My uncle and I	walk to the garden.
3 The ibika	follows us.
4 I	wrap bananas.
5 We	falls all day.
6 My cousin	sits and waits.
7 He	cooks the bananas.
8 Mother	cut the ripe bananas.

Unit 21

Making sentences interesting

Many of the words in a sentence tell more about the nouns, pronouns and verbs. We add other words to make the meaning clearer or the sentence more interesting. Example: *The boy hit a ball. The boy with short legs hit a ball made of tightly wound string. Her baby cries. Her sick baby cries without stopping.*

Activity A

Adjectives tell more about nouns and adverbs tell more about verbs. Example: *A small* (adjective) *boy hit a ball strongly* (adverb). Now, write these sentences. Add adjectives to tell more about the nouns, and adverbs to tell more about the verbs:

1 The teacher was writing.
2 A girl jumped over the fence.
3 The student cleaned the path.
4 A boy swept the classroom.
5 The carpenter fixed the door.
6 The woman cooks kaukau.

7 A girl finds a caterpillar.

8 The water is boiling.

9 The birds are eating the seeds.

10 The students learn the rules.

Activity B

Make more interesting sentences from the following sentences:

1 _____ and _____ ran along the beach. (add a subject of two nouns)

2 They ____ and ___ until late afternoon. (add two verbs)

3 They put the __________ and _________ that they found into their baskets. (add two nouns)

4 Suddenly the sky grew _________ and _______ . (add two adjectives)

5 They ran home ___________ (add one adverb)

6 The women cooked the _____, _____, _____food. (add three adjectives

Activity C

Here is a story. It needs adjectives and adverbs to make it more interesting. Write the story again with the new words.

I was on holiday. It was hot. We went to the bush. Mosquitoes bit us. My sister grumbled. We gathered breadfruit. The women got clay to make pots. It started to rain. Everyone complained. My father met us with the tractor. We rode home through the rain. The sun came out again. Mother roasted the breadfruit for dinner. The next day, we prepared the clay. The women beat the clay with wooden paddles. The men rolled the clay into coils and made pots. They drew designs and made handles. Later, when the pots were dry, they made a fire. They put the pots into the fire. We sold the pots at the market.

Unit 22

Parts of a sentence—clauses

Sentences are made up of groups of words that go together. A group of words with a subject and a verb is a *clause.*

Activity A

We can recognise a clause by finding its verb and its subject. Put a line under the *subjects* and a circle round the *verbs* in these sentences.

1 Giri paddles the canoe.
2 Sigin sits in the back.
3 They have fishing lines.
4 They are going to fish.
5 The sun is getting hot.
6 They are thirsty.
7 They have no water with them.
8 They go home.
9 They have not caught any fish.
10 Their mother is angry with them.

Activity B

Sentences can have more than one subject and more than one verb. Put a line under the *subjects* and a circle around the *verbs* in the following sentences. The number of clauses in each sentence is in the brackets. Example: My favourite reading book is an encyclopaedia because I like to find out facts. (2)

1 Our teacher likes setting homework everyday. (1)
2 I do homework because I like getting good grades. (2)
3 The homework was easy and I finished it quickly. (2)
4 I didn't finish the work so the teacher was angry. (2)
5 I read a lot because I like stories. (2)

Activity C

Every sentence must have at least one main clause. The main clause makes sense by itself. Example: *I hate homework.* (A single main clause is the sentence.) Are these main clauses? Put a tick if you think so:

1 I like projects.
2 I like reading books.
3 I enjoy assignments.
4 I prefer practical work.
5 I enjoy reading all kinds of books.

Activity D

Write five sentences that are made up of one main clause. The sentences should be about some part of your school life.

Activity E

A sentence can have two main clauses. Each main clause must make sense on its own and have a verb and a subject. Example: I hate homework but I like reading. I (subject) hate (verb) homework (main clause 1) but I (subject) like (verb) reading (main clause 2). Are there two main clauses in the following sentences? Put a tick if you think so.

1 I enjoy reading all kinds of books and I read everyday.
2 I like working in the school garden but I don't like helping with the chickens.

3 I do my homework on time so I get good marks.

4 I'm good at running and I like to win races.

5 I like to eat rice but I don't like to wash the rice pot.

Activity F

Put brackets around each of the main clauses in the sentences in Activity E. Example: (I do my homework on time) so (I get good marks).

Activity G

The words *and, but* and *so,* join the two main clauses in the sentences in Activity E. Write six sentences with two main clauses. Remember, each main clause must make sense by itself. Join the two main clauses with *and, but* or *so.*

Activity H

Some clauses do not make sense on their own. They have to be joined to a main clause. These clauses are called dependent clauses. Dependent clauses begin with words such as *because, until, although, unless, when, where, if, before.* Example: I was late because I did not get out of bed on time. Put a line under the dependent clause in each of the following sentences:

1 We worked hard *until* the teacher told us to stop.

2 I will need to read more books if I want to improve my reading.

3 I like reading books because they are interesting.

4 I enjoy weeding the garden unless it is hot.

5 I read the book when I was on holiday.

6 Her mother asked her where she had been.

Activity I

Write eight sentences with a main clause and a dependent clause using these words: *because, until, although, unless, when, where, if, before.*

Activity J

Some dependent clauses begin with *who, whose, that, which.* These dependent clauses add more information about the main clause. Example: *I like the woman who works in the store.* Put a line under the subordinate clauses in these sentences:

1 This is the story that I enjoyed the most.
2 I know whose book that is.
3 I admire students who study hard.
4 I read a book, which told me about our history.
5 I met the man who is coming to talk to our class.

Activity K

Add a main or a dependent clause to finish these sentences:

1 ... because it is a change from school. (main clause)
2 When I get a book I like, ... (main clause)
3 I will not go on the trip ... (dependent clause)
4 We were lost ... (dependent clause)
5 The truck broke down ... (dependent clause)

Unit 23

Parts of a sentence—phrases

Some groups of words in a sentence are called *phrases*. Phrases are different from clauses. Phrases do not have subjects or verbs. Phrases do not make sense by themselves. They are used to tell more about the clauses in a sentence. Example: *getting tired, on the table, at the beach, surprised by the dog.*

Activity A

Write if the group of words is a phrase. Example: *growing near the river* (phrase) *The breadfruit tree was growing near the river.* (not a phrase, it is a sentence)

1 My brother wrapped the bananas. __________

2 Clearing the weeds __________

3 The corn was ready. __________

4 Under the tree __________

5 With a bush knife __________

6 It was a long way from our house. __________

7 After the walk __________

8 We roasted some bananas before we walked home. __

9 We ate the bananas. __________

10 Before dark __________

Activity B

Put a line under the phrase in each sentence. Example: *The car ran off the road.*

1 Getting sleepy, I lay down.

2 A dog ran onto the road.
3 I put the plate on the table.
4 Surprised by the dog, I shouted.
5 Closing the door, I left the house.
6 I saw my father coming towards me.
7 I ran to the shops.
8 Finishing early, I went home.
9 We went to the beach.
10 My mother, tired by the long walk, slept near the fire.

Activity C

A phrase can start with a preposition. Example: *We carried the kaukau <u>to the house</u>. To* is a preposition. Put a line under the phrases starting with a preposition.

1 We hurried through the rain.
2 We made a shelter near the garden.
3 Mother left the baby in a bilum under the shelter.
4 The clouds went off towards the hills.
5 We weeded around the bananas.
6 I climbed up the tree.
7 I sat on a branch.
8 Mother cooked some greens over a small fire.
9 I sat down opposite her.
10 I ate cold rice from the saucepan.

Activity D

Write ten sentences of your own. The sentences should have a main clause and a phrase starting with a preposition. Example: *We hurried* (main clause) *through the rain* (phrase).

Activity E

A phrase can start with an *–ing* part of a verb. Example: *Feeling hungry.* The phrase does not make sense on its own. The phrase must be added to a clause: *Feeling hungry, we cooked some bananas over a fire.* Put a line under the phrase in each sentence:

1 Working hard, we finished the weeding.

2 Wrapping the bananas quickly, we worked together.

3 Smiling happily, they left for home.

4 Listening quietly, I heard the small frog.

5 Hurrying to get to school, I fell over.

6 Laughing loudly, the boy ran away.

7 Crying sadly, my grandfather visited his wife's grave.

8 Eating hungrily, my cousin soon finished all the food.

9 Standing near the door, I watched the video.

10 Eating greedily, the small dog growled at me.

Activity F

Write six sentences of your own starting with these phrases:

Laughing loudly, ...	Reading carefully, ...
Running quickly, ...	Closing my eyes, ...
Sweeping the floor, ...	Crying with fear, ...

Activity G

A phrase can start with the past form of the verb. Example: *Caught by the rain.* It is not a clause or a sentence, because it does not make sense on its own: The phrase must be added to a clause: *Caught by the rain, we ran for home.* Put a line under the phrase in each sentence:

1 Left alone, the baby began to cry.
2 Dug up, the peanuts dried in the sun.
3 Wet by the rain, the path was slippery.
4 Surprised by the noise, she jumped up.
5 Frightened of the snake, I ran away.
6 Trapped in the net, the bird tried to fly away.
7 Spilt by the dog, the water went across the floor.
8 Bent by the wind, the tree broke.
9 Called by her mother, the girl went home.
10 Burnt by the fire, the pot was spoilt.

Activity H

Write six sentences of your own starting with these phrases:

Worried about her father, ...	Left at the door, ...
Broken into little pieces, ...	Hurt by the knife, ...
Tied tightly, ...	Hung from the tree, ...

Unit 24

Questions beginning with question words

A question is a sentence that asks for an answer. Example: *Who is cooking? Is she cooking? Will she cook?* Some questions begin with question words such as *when, where, why, who, whose, what, which* and *how.*

Activity A

When questions ask about time. Example: *When did the boys weed the garden?* Write *when* questions using these ideas:

1 cut the grass (Answer: When did the boys cut the grass?)
2 return the library books
3 mend the desk
4 clean the blackboard
5 sweep the floor
6 feed the chickens

Activity B

Where questions ask about place. Example: *Where are the girls weeding?* Write *where* questions from these statements:

1 the boys cutting grass (Answer: Where are the boys cutting the grass?)
2 the teachers having a meeting
3 the girls gardening
4 the boys reading
5 the girls cooking
6 the teachers driving

Activity C

Why questions ask about reasons. Example: *Why are you late?* Write the rest of these *why* questions:

1 Why are you ...
2 Why did the ...
3 Why is he ...
4 Why are they ...
5 Why do you ...
6 Why has Tau ...
7 Why should I ...
8 Why was she ...

Activity D

Who questions ask about people. Example: *Who came to visit you last weekend?* Write five *who* questions of your own about last weekend.

Activity E

Whose questions ask about belonging. Example: *Whose cooking pots are those?* (The question is asking who the pots belong to.) Write five *whose* questions about these things:

1 Whose library books ...
2 Whose spade ...
3 Whose bush knife ...
4 Whose pencils ...
5 Whose bilum ...

Activity F

How questions ask about the way something is done, or the number. Example: *How can I travel? How many books are there?* Write these *how* questions:

How many ...	How much ...
How far ...	How did ...
How long ...	How often ...
How old ...	How is ...

Activity G

What questions ask for facts. Example: *What made you laugh?* Write these *what* questions:

What time ...	What will ...
What made ...	What is ...
What did ...	What food ...

Activity H

Which questions ask about things. Example: *Which truck was in the accident*? Write *which* questions about these ideas:

1 desk
2 window
3 broom
4 dormitory
5 bus

Unit 25

Questions beginning with verbs

Questions can begin with some verbs such as *do, be, will, can* and *have.*

Activity A

Some questions begin with *do, does* or *did.* Example: *Do you go hunting with your father? Does Tau go hunting with his father? Did they catch anything?* Follow the pattern and write a word to finish these questions:

1 Do	they	go	hunting?
2 Do	you	like	... ?
3 Does	Henao	know	... ?
4 Did	Veraga	visit	... ?
5 Do	the students	use	... ?
6 Does	she	remember	... ?

Activity B

Now write your own questions starting with *do, does* or *did.*

Follow the pattern in Activity A. (Make sure you use the correct form of the main verb such as *go, like, know, visit, use, remember.*)

Activity C

Some questions begin with forms of the verb, *to be: am, is, are, was or were*. Example: *Am I allowed to go too? Are you going anywhere special at the weekend? Is it going to rain? Were you pleased? Was the teacher happy?* Follow the pattern and finish these questions:

1 Was the teacher happy?
2 Were Vera and Gia ... ?
3 Was ... ?
4 Is ... ?
5 Are ... ?
6 Am I ... ?

Activity D

Now write your own questions. Follow the pattern in Activity C. Start your questions with *am, is, was, are* and *were*.

Activity E

Some helping verbs are used at the beginning of questions. Example: *Will you write to your pen friend? Can I go with you to the post office? Could we take Gabi's too? Should we let the teacher know we are going? Would we be able to go to the store too? Have you found that book?* Write your own questions beginning with these helping verbs:

1 Will ... ?
2 Can ... ?
3 Could ... ?
4 Should ... ?
5 Would ... ?
6 Have ... ?

Unit 26

Questions with *not*

Some questions begin with the verb plus *not.* Example: *Aren't you going home? Didn't you see that stone on the path?*

Activity A

Write a question to follow each pattern:

1 Don't you like reading?

2 ______________________________

3 Aren't you going home now?

4 ______________________________

5 Isn't that your friend coming?

6 ______________________________

7 Won't you come with me?

8 ______________________________

9 Didn't he bring something to eat?

10 ______________________________

Activity B

Change each of these questions into questions with *not.* Example: Do you like reading? *Don't you like reading?*

1 Does he like cutting grass?

2 Do you know where the spade is?

3 Is that your knife?

4 Are you going to Mendi?

5 Did you walk here?

Unit 27

Questions with tags

Sometimes, a statement is followed by a small question called a *question tag*. Example: *You won't be late* (statement), *will you?* (tag) *You will come on time* (statement), *won't you?* (tag)

Activity A

Match the statement and the tag. Example: *You won't touch the tools* (statement), *will you?* (tag)

Statement	Tag
1 You won't touch the tools,	were they?
2 You didn't take the spade,	did you?
3 Kaparu wasn't listening,	will you?
4 The spades weren't returned,	are you?
5 They haven't finished weeding,	will you?
6 You aren't very careful,	will I?
7 You won't forget,	was he?
8 I won't need a hat,	have they?

Activity B

Match the statement and the tag. Example: *You have got a library book* (statement), *haven't you?* (tag)

Statement	Tag
1 You have got a library book,	can't it?
2 I am careful,	haven't you?
3 A bush knife can be dangerous,	aren't I?
4 Kila and Siparu are careful,	wasn't I?
5 He could cut himself,	aren't they?
6 Katy must look after the knives,	couldn't he?
7 I was careless with the knife,	won't we?
8 We will go to Lae,	mustn't she?

Activity C

If *there* is the subject, the question tag must have *there.* Example: *There wasn't any need to worry, was there?* Write tags to finish these questions:

1 There are two books on the table, ... ?

2 There is a pencil on the floor, ... ?

3 There hasn't been any rain, ... ?

Activity D

If the statement does not have a helping verb such as *can* or *is,* we put *do* in the question tag. Example: *You like gardening, don't you?* Match these statements and tags:

1 I need a spade,	didn't he?
2 She reads a lot,	don't they?
3 He lost the knife,	don't we?
4 They like weeding,	don't I?
5 We play football well,	don't you?
6 You know the way home,	doesn't she?

Answers

Unit 1 Kinds of nouns

A 2. Gure, school 3. teacher, Independence 4. river, lake 5. hammer, box 6. Lina, clouds 7. Port Moresby, capital 8. waves, storm 9. highway, trucks 10. book, Monday

B 1. Simbu, Monday, Hani, Elizabeth, Toyota, New Ireland

C 1. grass, cloud, forest, pencil, shark, boy, paddle, cassowary, feather

D 1. justice, fear, violence, attention, freedom, independence, love 2. pain, joy, peace, excitement, kindness, patience

E 1. choir, congregation, flock, committee, queue 2. library, bunch/garland, herd, army, pack

Unit 2 Singular and plural nouns

F deer, feet, women, teeth, mice, lice, oxen, aircraft

G shells, houses, children, lollies, buses, wolves, dwarves, feathers, spoons, glasses, men

Unit 3 Nouns you can count and nouns you can't count

B 1. is 2. are 3. are 4. is 5. is 6. are 7. is 8. are 9. are 10. is 11. is 12. is 13. is 14. is 15. are

C 1. much 2. many 3. much 4. much 5. many 6. much 7. much 8. many 9. many 10. many 11. many 12. many 13. much 14. much 15. much

Unit 4 Pronouns

A 1. she 2. it 3. she 4. it 5. she

E 1. mine 2. theirs 3. ours 4. hers 5. his 6. yours

F 2. your pen 3. our classroom 4. his library book

5. our rubbish 6. their truck 7. her desk 8. my torn shirt
9. his pen 10. my rice 11. your plate 12. their coffee plantation

Unit 5 Using *I* and *me* correctly

A all are *I*

B all are *me*

Unit 6 Kinds of verbs

A 1. won 2. played 3. paddled 4. peeled 5. jumped 6. cleaned

B 1. spoke 2. hissed 3. warned 4. yelled 5. asked 6. laughed

C 1. worried 2. believed 3. enjoyed 4. knew 5. understood

D 1. am 2. is 3. is 4. is 5. are

E 1. have 2. have 3. has 4. has 5. has

Unit 7 Helping verbs

A 1. do 2. does 3. did 4. can 5. can 6. could 7. shall 8. should 9. should 10. will 11 would 12. would 13. am 14. are 15. is 16. was 17. were 18. have 19. has 20. had 21. am 22. can 23. was 24. are 25. could 26. were 27. shall 28. did 29. has 30. is

Unit 8 Verb tenses

A 1. read 2. likes 3. eat 4. plays 5. sees 6. thanks 7. barks 8. travels 9. walk 10. stops

B 1. kicked 2. stopped 3. slipped 4. called 5. cheered 6. barked 7. stirred 8. addressed 9. thanked 10. watched

C 1. will drink 2. will copy 3. will reply 4. will wake 5. will tell 6. will drop 7. will ring 8. will speak

Unit 9 Using *has*, *have* and *had* with verbs

A 1. have finished 2. have covered 3. have planted 4. has asked 5. have washed 6. have walked 7. have returned 8. has talked 9. have copied 10 has packed

B 1. had harvested 2. had picked 3. had washed 4. had finished 5. had started 6. had planted 7. had walked 8. had played 9. had worried 10. had rained

Unit 10 Using -ing verbs

A 1. are drawing 2. am watching 3. is folding 4. are scraping 5. is sitting

B 1. is sitting 2. are (you) doing 3. am washing 4. is (your sister) helping 5. she's sitting

C 1. was sitting 2. was watching 3. was resting 4. was washing 5. was asking 6. was doing 7. were sitting 8. was coming

Unit 11 Making the nouns and verbs agree

A 1. go 2. feels 3. catches 4. think 5. speeds 6. look 7. shines 8. stop 9. make 10. throw 11. pull 12 feels

B 1. are 2. am 3. has 4. Does 5. Are 6. haven't 7. have 8. am 9. are 10. have 11. is 12. are

Unit 12 Irregular verbs

A 1. I speak, she speaks, I spoke, I will speak, I have spoken
2. I catch, she catches, I caught, I will catch, I have caught
3. I cut, she cuts, I cut, I will cut, I have cut
4. I write, she writes, I wrote, I will write, I have written

B come, came, have come; see, saw, have seen; bend, bent, have bent; feel, felt, have felt; kneel, knelt, have knelt; leave, left, have left; sleep, slept, have slept; shut, shut, have shut; show, showed, have shown; buy, bought, have bought; bring, brought, have brought; freeze, froze, have frozen; forget, forgot, have forgotten

C 1. found 2. have forgotten 3. came 4. saw 5. shut 6. thought

D 2. was 3. was 4. will be 5. am 6. is 7. were 8. were 9. are 10. will be 11. was 12. will be 13. was 14. will be 15. were

Unit 13 Adjectives

B 2. sandy path 3. delicious scones 4. traditional trade 5. old man, stone axes 6. ripe mango, hard ground 7. heavy bilum, cut firewood 8. large gardens 9. salty soup 10. north wind, heavy rain

Unit 14 Comparing using adjectives

A 1. longer 2. faster 3. slower 4. smoother 5. louder

B 1. more tiring 2. more slippery 3. more dangerous 4. more enormous 5. more puzzled

C 1. the thinnest 2. the wisest 3. the prettiest 4. the strongest 5. the cleverest 6. the noisiest

D 1. the most intelligent 2. the most beautiful 3. the most powerful 4. the most wonderful 5. the most handsome 6. the most honest

Unit 15 Adverbs

A 1. slowly 2. always 3. quickly 4. badly 5. early 6. softly 7. everywhere 8. sometimes

Unit 16 Prepositions

B beside, between, near, through, among, behind, outside

C during, for the whole day, until, then, before, for a week

D 1. in 2. during 3. at night 4. then 5. by 6. since 7. beneath 8. across 9. from 10. before

Unit 17 Connecting words

A and, so, but, or

C 1. or 2. but 3. but 4. and 5. and

D 1. because 2. before 3. since 4. so that 5. unless

E 1. We go to the beach everyday unless it rains.
2. We are happy if the weather is fine.
3. We walk to the beach after we have breakfast.
4. We hurry so that we'll have more time at the beach.
5. My oldest sister comes too because she needs to look after us.
6. We stay at the beach until it gets dark.

Unit 18 What is a sentence?

A 1. yes 2. no 3. yes 4. yes 5. no 6. yes 7. no 8. no 9. yes 10. yes 11. no 12. no 13. yes 14. no 15. yes

B 1. I don't like it when you are angry/When you are angry I don't like it.
2. She waited at the gate.
3. Look out for the crocodile!
4. We like going on the bus.

5. My mother cooks delicious food. 6. I like to play with my dog. 7. Get off the bus where the road ends. 8. He is going home. 9. I have a new pen friend 10. I sat under the mango tree.

Unit 19 Kinds of sentences

B 1. Is Tau's dog old?
2. Does Gia live there?
3. Does Lohia read a lot?
4. Is the bus late?
5. Is the food ready?
6. Are you frightened?
7. Do you eat tin fish?
8. Do you like mangoes?

E 1. question 2. statement 3. statement 4. order 5.exclamation 6. request 7. question 8. exclamation 9. order 10. question

Unit 20 The two parts of sentences

A 1. yes 2. no 3. no 4. yes 5. no 6. yes 7. yes 8. no

B 2. birds (subject) were calling (verb) 3. butterflies (subject) flew (verb) 4. a bird of paradise (subject) was singing (verb) 5. rain (subject) started (verb) 6. we (subject) ran (verb) 7. the stream (subject) was (verb) 8. the path (subject) was (verb)

C 1. The rain falls all day.
2. My uncle and I walk to the garden.
3. The ibika is ready.
4. I wrap bananas.
5. We cut the ripe bananas.
6. My cousin follows us.
7. He sits and waits./He cooks the bananas.
8. Mother cooks the bananas./He cooks the bananas./He sits and waits./Mother sits and waits.

Unit 22 Parts of a sentence—clauses

A 2. Sigin sits 3. They have 4. They are 5. The sun is 6. They are 7. They have 8. They go 9. They have 10. Their mother is

B 1. Our teacher likes 2. I do, I like 3. The homework was, I finished 4. I didn't finish, the teacher was 5. I read, I like

C all are main clauses

E all sentences have two main clauses

F 1. (I enjoy reading all kinds of books) and (I read everyday).
2. (I like working in the school garden) but (I don't like helping with the chickens).
3. (I do my homework on time) so (I get good marks).
4. (I'm good at running) and (I like to win races).
5. (I like to eat rice) but (I don't like to wash the rice pot).

H 2. if I want to improve my reading 3. because they are interesting 4. unless it is hot 5. when I was on holiday 6. where she had been

J 1. that I enjoyed the most 2. whose book that is 3. who study hard 4. which told me about our history 5. who is coming to talk to our class

Unit 23 Parts of a sentence—phrases

A 1. sentence 2. phrase 3. sentence 4. phrase 5. phrase 6. sentence 7. phrase 8. sentence 9. sentence 10. phrase

B 1. Getting sleepy 2. onto the road 3. on the table 4. Surprised by the dog 5. Closing the door 6. towards me 7. to the shops 8. Finishing early 9. to the beach 10. tired by the long walk

C 1. through the rain 2. near the garden 3. in a bilum under the shelter 4. towards the hills 5. around the bananas 6. up the tree 7. on a branch 8. over a small fire 9. opposite her 10. from the saucepan

E 1. Working hard 2. Wrapping the bananas quickly 3. Smiling happily 4. Listening quietly 5. Hurrying to get to school 6. Laughing loudly 7. Crying sadly 8. Eating hungrily 9. Standing near the door 10. Eating greedily

G 1. Left alone 2. Dug up 3. Wet by the rain 4. Surprised by the noise 5. Frightened of the snake 6. Trapped in the net 7. Spilt by the dog 8. Bent by the wind 9. Bent by the wind 10. Burnt by the fire

Unit 24 Questions beginning with question words

A 2. When did the boys return the library books?
3. When did the girls mend the desk?
4. When did the boys clean the blackboard?
5. When did the boys sweep the floor?
6. When did the girls feed the chickens?

B 2. Where are the teachers having a meeting?
3. Where are the girls gardening?
4. Where are the boys reading?
5. Where are the girls cooking?
6. Where are the teachers driving

E 1. Whose library books are those?
2. Whose spade is that?
3. Whose bush knife is that?
4. Whose pencils are those?
5. Whose bilum is that?

Unit 26 Questions with *not*

B 1. Doesn't he like cutting grass?
2. Don't you know where the spade is?
3. Isn't that your knife?
4. Aren't you going to Mendi?
5. Didn't you walk here?

Unit 27 Questions with tags

A 2. You didn't take the spade, did you?
3. Kaparu wasn't listening, was he?
4. The spades weren't returned, were they?
5. They haven't finished weeding, have they?
6. You aren't very careful, are you?
7. You won't forget, will you?
8. I won't need a hat, will I?

B 2. I am careful, aren't I?
3. A bush knife can be dangerous, can't it?
4. Kila and Siparu are careful, aren't they?
5. He could cut himself, couldn't he?
6. Katy must look after the knives, mustn't she?
7. I was careless with the knife, wasn't I?
8. We will go to Lae, won't we?

C 1. There are two books on the table, aren't there?
2. There is a pencil on the floor, isn't there?
3. There hasn't been any rain, has there?

D 1. I need a spade, don't I?
2. She reads a lot, doesn't she?
3. He lost the knife, didn't he?
4. They like weeding, don't they?
5. We play football well, don't we?
6. You know the way home, don't you?